SAVING THE TASMANIAN DEVIL

How Science Is Helping the World's Largest Marsupial Carnivore Survive

Dorothy Hinshaw Patent

Houghton Mifflin Harcourt
Boston   New York

For my friend and colleague Jenny Marshall Graves, who inspired me to bring this fascinating story to young readers.

The text type was set in Albany Std.
The display type was set in Shaky Hand Some Comic and Family Cat Fat.

Library of Congress Cataloging-in-Publication Data

Names: Patent, Dorothy Hinshaw, author.
Title: Saving the Tasmanian devil : how science is helping the world's largest marsupial carnivore survive / Dorothy Hinshaw Patent.
Other titles: Scientists in the field.
Description: New York, New York : Houghton Mifflin Harcourt, [2019] | Series: Scientists in the field | Audience: Ages 10-12. | Audience: Grades 4 to 6.
Identifiers: LCCN 2018034813 | ISBN 9780544991484 (hardcover)
Subjects: LCSH: Tasmanian devil--Diseases--Juvenile literature. | Epidemics--Australia--Tasmania--Juvenile literature. | Tumors--Juvenile literature. | Genetic disorders--Juvenile literature. | Wildlife conservation--Australia--Tasmania--Juvenile literature. | Wildlife rescue--Australia--Tasmania--Juvenile literature. | Tasmania--Juvenile literature.
Classification: LCC QL737.M33 P38 2019 | DDC 599.2/7--dc23
LC record available at https://lccn.loc.gov/2018034813

Manufactured in China
SCP 10 9 8 7 6 5 4 3 2 1
4500759104

A curious young devil.

CONTENTS

Tasmania is a beautiful island with lots of wild land.

Prologue

March 7, 2015: I'm joined by my college friend Jenny Marshall Graves and her daughter, Erica, for a stroll along a California beach. We had lots to catch up on after fifty years apart. Jenny had become a widely respected geneticist, specializing in the chromosomes of native animals in Australia, her home country. She told me of her role in the scientific race to save the Tasmanian devil, the largest native Australian carnivore, from extinction. A strange and fatal disease called Devil Facial Tumor Disease (DFTD) had shown up out of nowhere and was sweeping across Tasmania, an island off the coast of mainland Australia and the home of these animals. The disease moved so fast that some scientists feared the species would be wiped out in the wild within twenty years.

As Jenny related the timeline of DFTD across Tasmania and the efforts of scientists to grasp what was happening, I became captivated by the story. Where had the disease come from? How did it spread? What was the cause—bacteria? Viruses? And could it be stopped?

In response to my many questions, Jenny said, "Why don't you come to Australia to find out for yourself? I can connect you with other scientists involved, and you can stay with my family when you're in Melbourne."

How could I resist her generous offer? I jumped at it, and my husband, Greg, and I headed "down under" at the end of August the following year.

When Jenny described the situation, it seemed straightforward—DFTD was sweeping across Tasmania, and the devils in the wild would all be gone within a decade or two. Scientists hoped that they could then repopulate Tasmania with devils from captive populations. During my journey of discovery, however, I ended up witnessing enough twists and turns in this complicated and evolving story as in any fine whodunit.

Scientists Tackling DFTD

It takes many scientists in several different fields of work to figure out how to combat a problem like Devil Facial Tumor Disease. I've chosen these four, since each has focused on different ways to investigate the disease in hopes of uncovering its secrets and helping the Tasmanian devil survive.

Jenny Marshall Graves, Geneticist

After earning her PhD in molecular biology at the University of California, Berkeley, Jenny returned to Australia with her American husband, John.

Jenny believes that investigating the genetics of less-studied animals, from kangaroos to emus to Tasmanian devils, is vital to understanding genetics in general. During her long career she has analyzed the genomes of many species, including platypuses and dragon lizards. She has received international recognition for her research and, in 2017, she received the Australian Prime Minister's Prize for Science, a great honor.

Menna Jones, Ecologist

Menna has always loved fieldwork—getting out into the wild to study how nature works. Her PhD work at the University of Tasmania focused on the biological family of predatory marsupials that includes Tasmanian devils and quolls and how changes in the biological environment affect the populations of different species. Menna had been studying the devils for years before the appearance of DFTD, providing background data on what things were like before DFTD came along and changed everything.

Jenny Graves receiving the Australian Prime Minister's Prize for Science in 2017 with Australian Senator Michaelia Cash and Prime Minister Malcolm Turnbull.

Jenny enjoys an up-close and personal visit with a baby devil.

Menna Jones with a healthy devil caught in one of her traps.

She and her colleagues continue to study wild devils to increase the understanding of their behavior and ecological needs.

Greg Woods, Cancer Researcher

"I've always been interested in cancer and had lofty ambitions of working on a project that cured the disease," Greg explains. After receiving his PhD from the University of Tasmania, he spent time in Toronto, Canada, then returned to the Menzies Institute for Medical Research at the University of Tasmania to continue his research on leukemia and to teach immunology, or how immune systems fight disease. He says that when he learned about DFTD, "it seemed that destiny had determined that my research would focus on the immune escape mechanisms of DFTD."

Greg is now semiretired, but studies at the Menzies Institute continue, as students and other researchers work

Greg Woods takes a break from his work in the laboratory.

on different aspects of DFTD and the immune system in order to understand this complex disease and find ways to prevent it.

Alex Fraik, Graduate Student in Genomics

Researchers at Washington State University in Pullman, Washington, such as Alex Fraik, collaborate with researchers at the University of

Alex Fraik holds a Tasmanian devil caught in one of her traps.

Tasmania, including Menna Jones, on vital studies of DFTD and how the devils and the disease are changing as they interact with one another and with the environment. Along with other students at both universities, Alex focuses her research on how Tasmanian devils are adapting to the challenge of DFTD by studying how their genetics have changed since the disease appeared. Alex wants to help inspire young people who care about the environment and the future of our planet to become scientists.

CHAPTER ONE

The Unfolding of a Disaster

In 1996, photographer Christo Baars snapped some disturbing Tasmanian devil images in northeastern Tasmania. The faces of the devils that he captured on film were hideously distorted. He'd never seen anything like it. His friend, government zoologist Nick Mooney, passed the photos on to his colleagues, who hadn't seen such damaged devils before either. Perhaps this was a cancer caused by some environmental factor, they thought.

Fast-forward to 1999. Tasmanian ecologist Menna Jones, who hadn't heard about Christo's photos from three years before, checked some traps she'd set in the wild for Tasmanian devils. Moving along the trapline, she was shocked. "As I got closer to the northern end of the trapline," Menna says, "I saw that about a third of the devils had these horrendous growths on their heads. I didn't have a camera with me and I didn't collect samples. I just didn't have time to follow it up right away." Menna continues, "In 2001, I trapped three devils with the huge tumors and took photos. I was the first biologist to see and then photograph the disease in the wild."

From then on, Menna kept track of the horror's spread. "In January 2002, I picked up the disease 6.2 miles [10 kilometers] south of the previous finds, giving us the first data that showed the disease was spreading." Then, in July 2002, only six months later, Menna saw a 60 percent drop in the devil population; where she had once trapped sixty animals, she now found only fourteen. And nearly all the adults she found had the disease. In 2003, Menna's colleague

Two curious young devils check out visitors at Trownna Wildlife Preserve on Tasmania.

Menna Jones carries her son Mungo on her back and devil traps in her hands as she wades ashore to catch devils.

One of Menna's photos of a devil with DFTD.

Nick Mooney found very few devils in the northeast. The whole area seemed to have lost its devils. Nick Mooney and Dr. Marco Resani also found that the disease had spread widely in the center and east of the island.

Farmers were also reporting that fewer devils seemed to be around. Devils hunt prey, but they are also excellent scavengers, and the carcasses of dead sheep and cows on northeastern farms were often untouched. By then it was clear that the disease somehow passed from one animal to another, it was spreading fast, and it was deadly. What was going on?

By 2003, scientists had named the plague "Devil Facial Tumor Disease." In 2004, the Australian and Tasmanian governments set up the Save the Tasmanian Devil Program, which in 2005 began capturing animals from areas that were still free of disease to create "insurance populations" in zoos and wildlife parks. If scientists' worst fears were realized and the disease wiped out all the wild devils, then these captive animals, or their future offspring, might be released into the wild so they could repopulate Tasmania. Research also intensified into how devils live in the wild and into whether a vaccine could be developed to protect them from the disease.

Their concern was warranted—devil populations plunged by as much as 95 percent in areas the disease reached, which included most of Tasmania. The disease seemed to be 100 percent fatal. But until scientists knew the cause, how could they find an effective treatment or know how to protect animals from becoming infected?

EASTERN
AUSTRALIA

Kuranda • Cairns

QUEENSLAND

Toowoomba • Brisbane
Gold Coast

NEW SOUTH
WALES

Sydney •

Adelaide •

CANBERRA ★

VICTORIA

Melbourne • Healesville

Launceston •
TASMANIA

Hobart •

The places Dorothy visited along Australia's east coast on her quest
to learn about the devil are shown in red on this map.

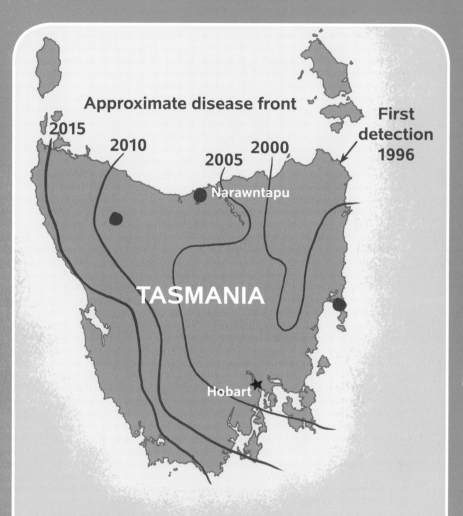

Approximate disease front

2015
2010
2005   2000
First
detection
1996

Narawntapu

TASMANIA

Hobart ★

Since 1996, an infectious facial tumor that kills Tasmanian
devils has spread across Tasmania. DNA from three devil
populations (red circles) suggests that some animals
carry genetic resistance to the disease.

Finding the Cause

Jenny Graves's phone rang in the winter of 2005 (summer in the Northern Hemisphere). On the other end was fellow geneticist Anne-Maree Pearse from Hobart, Tasmania. "I'd like to see what you think of my photographs of Tasmanian devil tumor cells. Could I come and see you? Don't tell anyone," she said.

"I was intrigued," Jenny said. "I'd never looked at devil chromosomes, but I knew they were just about the same across many related species."

A few days later, Anne-Maree arrived at Jenny's lab. Jenny recalls, "She spread out her karyotypes [chromosome photographs taken using a microscope] of chromosomes of both normal animals and animals with the tumors. When I looked at her images, I nearly fell off my chair. The tumor chromosomes were weird, containing one superlong chromosome, and with no sign of sex chromosomes. Weird chromosomes are quite standard for solid tumors in humans. The amazing thing about these was that the chromosomes from tumors from different animals were all the same!"

Anne-Maree confirmed that, yes, the chromosomes were from tumors found in different devils, even though they all looked the same.

"You may think I'm crazy," Jenny said to Anne-Maree, "but I think you must have a cell clone."

Jenny explained to me, "I realized that somehow a devil tumor cell was jumping from one animal to another. *Not* a virus or a bacterium. This was an unprecedented concept, but there was really no other explanation.

Anne-Maree was very receptive to the idea; I think she'd already come to this conclusion but needed confirmation."

Anne-Maree and her assistant, Kate Swift, published their discovery in 2006, proposing that one animal had developed the cancerous tumor. Normally the immune system of another animal would recognize the tumor cells as "other," coming from a different individual, and destroy them. But somehow, these cells were able to establish themselves and grow into deadly tumors that could then be passed on to other unfortunate devils through biting.

What I learned: The cause of DFTD is a kind of cancer seen only once before, as a rare tumor in female dogs. Cancerous cells from one animal are passed on to another animal by physical contact. The second animal's body does not recognize that the tumor cells are not its own cells, so these diseased cells infect the victim and grow. Scientists are studying the chromosomes of diseased devils to learn how they differ from the chromosomes of normal devils.

Chromosomes and Cancer

The genes in the cells of most living things are made of DNA. DNA molecules are arranged in paired structures called "chromosomes" in the nucleus (the central part) of the cell. One chromosome in each pair is inherited from the female parent. The other chromosome comes from the male parent.

Different species have different numbers of chromosome pairs. Humans have twenty-three sets of pairs; Tasmanian devils have just seven. Most of the time, the DNA that carries the inherited traits of an organism is loosely arranged in the cell's nucleus. But when the cell divides, the DNA strands clump together in an orderly fashion into chromosomes that you can see with a microscope. Then each chromosome is duplicated and the cell divides in two, with one copy of each chromosome going into each of the two new cells. That way, one cell becomes two identical cells.

Human Male

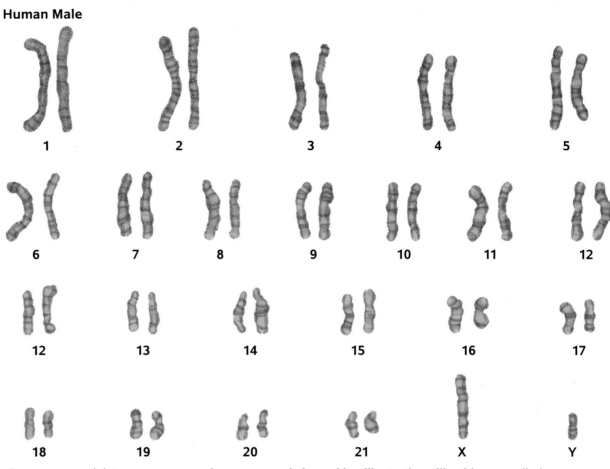

One way geneticists can compare chromosomes is by making illustrations like this one called "karyotypes." The chromosomes are imaged when a cell is getting ready to divide, then cut out and rearranged into an image in which the sets of numbered pairs are lined up in a row. This method allows comparisons of one organism with another in the same species to see if there are visible differences between them.

Normal cells grow and divide until the body reaches the number of cells of that type that are needed. Then they stop dividing. Cancer cells just keep growing and dividing and don't stop. They are relentless. It's difficult to identify which genes are responsible for turning a normal cell into a cancer cell because many different genes can be involved, depending on the cell type and the organism.

One way a cell can become cancerous is when mistakes occur during the copying of the DNA in the chromosomes during cell division. Another way is when the arrangement of the genes on the chromosome inadvertently gets altered. These mistakes can result in changes in how the genes function. For example, a change in a chromosome could change the order of the genes so that a gene that controls growth could end up right next to a gene that promotes that activity. The cells with this new arrangement of genes could end up dividing with no letup, resulting in a cancer.

Major changes in chromosomes can be seen under a microscope. Geneticists, the scientists who study genetics, or how traits are passed from one generation to another, can label the chromosome pairs during cell division with special chemical stains to see what they look like. The chromosomes from normal cells of any particular species look the same, except for the sex chromosomes. In humans and in Tasmanian devils,

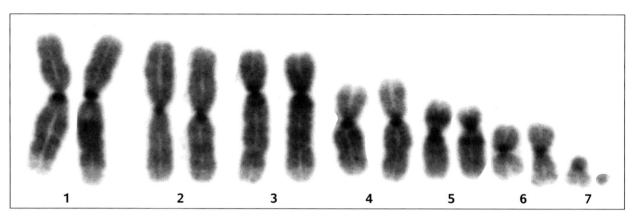

This image shows the karyotype of a normal Tasmanian devil cell. Each pair of chromosomes is numbered from left to right. The last pair is the sex chromosomes. Since this karyotype is from a male devil, it has one X and one smaller Y chromosome.

for example, females have two X chromosomes, while males have one X and one Y.

When scientists prepare and stain the chromosomes from a devil facial tumor, it is clear that they look totally different from chromosomes in normal cells. The biggest change is in chromosome number 1, which no longer exists as a pair but has been broken into pieces and moved around. Most of the other chromosomes have also changed. This diagram shows the changes in detail.

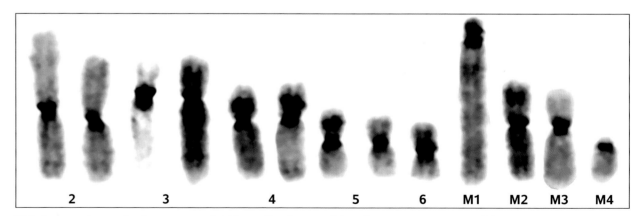

This image shows the karyotype of DFTD cells. Some of the chromosomes, especially the #1 pair and the #7 (X pair) have been badly broken up. Pairs numbered 2–6, except for one missing #5 can still be recognized, but as you can see in the diagram on page 15, bits of some chromosomes have moved.

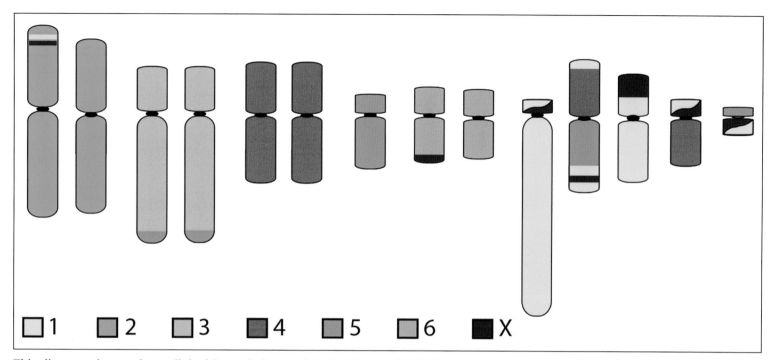

This diagram shows where all the bits and pieces of the broken-up devil chromosomes have gone. This kind of disarray of chromosomes is typical of cancer cells. You can see that most of chromosome 1 is now in the long extra piece, which also has a bit of the X chromosome. One chromosome 5 has disappeared, and the extra pieces have parts of chromosomes 1, 4, 5, and X.

One chromosome in the number 2 pair has a tiny piece from number 1 and a bit from the X chromosome. Each number 3 chromosome has a bit from number 5. One number 6 has a small piece of the X, and one number 5 has been broken up completely. Instead of normal chromosome number ones, there are chromosome pieces that have genes from other pairs of chromosomes.

Somehow, these changes have resulted in cancer cells, cells that just keep dividing and dividing until they take over and kill the host.

CHAPTER TWO
Life of the Devil

No wonder DFTD can devastate a devil population quickly—biting and threatening to bite are a big part of a Tasmanian devil's life. Not only does a devil have arguably the most powerful bite of any mammal its size, but it uses that bite for more than just cracking down on bones and ripping through the often tough skin of its food. Devils bite and posture to bite to threaten other devils that might want to share in their road-kill or in mating behavior.

This distinctive carnivore once inhabited the Australian mainland but was wiped out there at least a thousand years ago. It survived a little longer than its larger distant cousin, the thylacine or Tasmanian tiger, which was named for the stripes or bands along the back part of its body. Extinction on Tasmania followed for the thylacine. It was shot, trapped, and poisoned as an enemy of sheep farmers. This left the much smaller devil as the largest living carnivorous marsupial.

This captive devil is more likely to be yawning than threatening to bite.

The Tasmanian devil has become a symbol of Tasmania. The devil got its name in the early 1800s, when the first English settlers arrived. Imagine being one of those settlers. Darkness falls over your campsite and you are trying to sleep, when suddenly you hear mysterious, frightening sounds—unearthly screams and shrieks echoing through the forest. The sounds alone frighten you, but then you see movement in the moonlight—a black creature disappearing into the night. You believe in the existence of the devil, and you know that night is the time for terrifying creatures like werewolves and vampires, so why not a devil as well?

Like most Australian mammals, the Tasmanian devil is a marsupial. A marsupial's young develop in a pouch on their mother's belly rather than in a uterus inside their mother's body.

The devil is only about the size of a small dog. Its body is stocky, with short legs and a thick tail. Like most Australian animals, wild devils tend to be active from dusk to dawn. They make secluded dens or take over dens made by other animals, such as wombats, and usually spend the daylight hours inside. The devil runs with a unique loping gait that

it can maintain for long distances while hunting, patrolling the edges between forests and fields and along paths and trails where its prey passes at night. Unfortunately, the devil's habit of naturally traveling along trails and paths as well as eating roadkill and other carrion means that devils often become roadkill in their quest for food.

Despite its portrayal in cartoons, a real Tasmanian devil is not destructive and crazy; its nocturnal and generally solitary lifestyle left it vulnerable to the imagination of Hollywood animators.

It's easy for devils to tear apart the carcass of a dead animal using their powerful jaws and sharp teeth.

Devils have short legs and wide bodies.

Devils have a unique running gait but can run for long distances without tiring.

Devil Stats

Scientific Name: *Sarcophilus harrisii*

Color: Black, usually with patches of white on the chest and rump

Size: Males usually larger than females. Females generally weigh 14 to 18 pounds (6 to 8 kilograms) and males up to 28 pounds (13 kilograms). Adults have a combined head and body length of 19 to 28 inches (500 to 710 millimeters); their tail is 9 to 12 inches (240 to 310 millimeters).

Life Span: 4 to 6 years in the wild, a little longer in captivity

Reproduction: Devils usually mate in March. A female carries up to four young in her pouch, which opens facing backward (the pouches of many marsupials, such as kangaroos, open at the top or front). The young become independent at 9 to 10 months old.

This male devil was the largest Menna has ever caught.

Since Australia is in the Southern Hemisphere, its seasons are reversed from those in the Northern Hemisphere. Spring runs from September through November; summer is December through February; fall is March through May; winter is June through August. Devils mate in the fall, and the male bites the female often during mating, also grabbing her by the neck and dragging her into his den to keep her away from other males. The tiny young are born three weeks after mating. Up to four of them attach to the teats inside their

This young devil is just getting brave enough to leave the den.

mother's pouch and grow there until they are fully furred at sixteen weeks. Then they stay in the den while their mother hunts. As they get older, they begin to venture out into the world until they are on their own by nine or ten months old.

What I learned:
Tasmanian devils and Tasmanian tigers once lived on the Australian mainland but became extinct there long ago. The Tasmanian tiger became extinct in Tasmania in the twentieth century, leaving the devil as the largest carnivorous marsupial in the world.

These two young devils are enjoying the sunshine just outside their den entrance.

Native to Australia

Australia has been isolated from other landmasses for many thousands of years—long enough for a whole different assortment of plants and animals to evolve there. The biggest difference is in its mammals, animals that have hair and produce milk to feed their young. Almost all mammals on other continents are placental mammals, meaning that their young grow in the uterus inside the mother's body and get their nutrients through an organ called a placenta. With the exception of bats, rodents, and marine mammals, the only native Australian mammals are either marsupials or monotremes (egg-laying mammals). Instead of developing inside a uterus in the mother's body, when marsupial young are born, they are tiny and pink and not fully developed. They crawl into the pouch on their mother's belly, where they latch onto a nipple that provides them with milk so they can grow and develop. As many as twenty tiny Tasmanian devil young are born to each mother in March and April. The mother, however, has just four nipples, so only four of those babies will be able to receive nourishment and grow in her pouch.

Kangaroos, wallabies, koalas, wombats—all of these are marsupials native to Australia. Opossums are the only native marsupials in North and

You can see how tiny baby devils are when they are born. These four tiny, pink week-old devils all fit on a coin smaller than a quarter.

The young devils stay in their mother's pouch until they have grown their fur coats and become quite large.

Koalas spend most of their time in trees, feeding on eucalyptus leaves.

South America, and no wild marsupials naturally inhabit the continents of Europe, Asia, and Africa.

The most unusual Australian mammals are the monotremes. Only two kinds of monotremes exist today: the echidna, also called a spiny anteater, and the platypus. Unlike other mammals, monotremes lay eggs in hidden nests. Monotreme mothers have milk glands on their bellies, and when their eggs hatch, the young lap up the milk as it is secreted.

The echidna is a monotreme, a very unusual mammal that actually lays eggs.

These two devils at the Healesville Sanctuary are curious about visitors.

CHAPTER THREE
Meeting the Devil

My first devil encounter is unexpected. My husband and I begin our Australian adventures in the Daintree Rainforest near the northeastern town of Cairns. We visit a small zoo, and just as we enter, we see a small pen that serves as home to a captive devil. Adapted to having the freedom to run long distances, this devil can only run on the hardened ground of a path he forged by running, running, running around and around, only stopping to sleep, eat, or drink. Confinement caused this obsessive behavior. A zoo guide shares that every once in a while the devil stops and spins around in a circle a few times, then he continues his endless running. One morning keepers found him bleeding from bite wounds he'd made on his own body. I stop for a moment as the group of visitors walks away to the next attraction. I lean toward the devil's fence. He sees me, stops his running, and comes over for a brief moment to look at me. He then resumes his hypnotic circling.

This lone devil spends its life running around and around in its small enclosure.

Australia is home to many beautiful birds, like this parrot.

September is springtime in Australia, and Jenny enjoys picking asparagus in her garden.

After enjoying snorkeling along the Great Barrier Reef and visiting local farms in the northeast, I'm eager to visit Jenny and her family and begin learning more about devils firsthand. We fly south to Melbourne, where Jenny and her husband, John, pick us up at the airport and take us to their home in the suburb of Eltham.

Jenny has news for me about the Tasmanian devil. First is the good news: Menna Jones and her colleagues are still finding healthy devils in small numbers, even in the area where DFTD first appeared—maybe the species is already developing immunity to the disease and evolving to survive it. The other news, not as good, is that another facial tumor disease has popped up in the southeastern part of the island. The first disease originated in what's called a Schwann cell in a female devil. Schwann cells wrap around nerves to help insulate them. This new form of the disease is in a different cell type and was found in a male devil. I'd arrived in Australia to research a simple story, a fatal disease that was wiping out wild Tasmanian devils, but things are already getting more complicated.

After a day in town, we drive to a spacious zoo in the countryside

The pens used for the breeding devils in the insurance population at Healesville are quite spacious.

called the Healesville Sanctuary, a center for the Tasmanian devil insurance-population program.

Kathy Starr, the senior keeper in charge of the program, guides us as we ride through this property that is devoted to seven breeding pens. I smell the sweet wild air and savor the frequent birdcalls that penetrate the peaceful silence. The staff enjoys working in this area because it's so quiet and out of the way.

One very important goal of this program is to keep the animals as wild as possible. Each fenced enclosure contains about .7 acres (.28 hectares) and is heavily vegetated. If there's a tree near the fence, it's covered with slick plastic so the devils can't climb it and jump out. Cameras inside track movement, and each pen has an automatic watering system. Food is brought in by trucks during the daytime, while the devils are asleep, and left for each animal. They are fed their natural diet of wild prey such as wallabies, possums, fish, and eggs. (Devils can climb trees and young devils will raid birds' nests.) The keepers stay out of sight. Kathy points out that the devils growing up in Healesville may be released into the wild, so it's vital that they don't get used to humans.

After touring the breeding-pen area, we meet with devil keeper Peter Comber, who describes the care procedures for the insurance-population devils. The keepers maintain detailed records on all the animals and do everything they can to ensure their health, like checking the enclosures two or three times a day to see if the food is gone and the animals have defecated. When mating season arrives, a male and a female are placed in side-by-side pens and their behavior is watched for several nights to see if they are interested in each other. If things look promising, the gate between the pens is opened and the animals' behavior is carefully watched. It's important for the male devil to be dominant and not let the female bully him.

A camera in the den allows the keepers and other staff to verify mating. Fifty-five days after mat-

The webcams keep track of activity in the dens. Here a mother devil interacts with her youngsters.

ing, the keepers check the female's pouch for young. After the offspring successfully leave the pouch, the den camera follows every activity of the mother and her babies. We look at the screen that displays the den camera to find a cozy scene of the mother and her two youngsters shifting around in the near darkness.

We visit the devil's area in the public part of the zoo next. One exhibit features a single male devil; the other, three females. All four are too old to breed, so now they are ambassadors for their species. The male acts shy, peeking out from inside a hollow log.

Two of the females are quite curious about us. First Tierney comes up near the fence, then Sassafrass, both sniffing and looking up at us as they bob their heads.

Peter then shows us cards they have identifying all of the more than 150 devils that have been at Healesville. Each card gives the animal's name, gender, sire (father), and dam (mother) on one side and has draw-

Here is one side of Tierney's card and the other side of Sassafrass's card; the black and white markings are shown in reverse on all the cards. The symbol in red indicates that this animal is a female.

The male devil is kept in his own pen, since males in captivity often don't get along well with other devils.

B10701

Sassafrass

D8D7- Trovan
Dam: Pheonix
Sire: Bruce

Tierney

ings showing its markings on the other side.

It's lunchtime, and Jenny, Greg, and I join reproductive biologist Marissa Parrott in the café. Marissa tells us that Healesville is one of thirty-eight zoos and wildlife parks in Australia that has captive devils. Some zoos are small and have only retired breeding animals that help educate the public about the devils' plight. Healesville, however, serves several goals. The animals in the display area advance public education, and the ones used in breeding are sometimes also important research subjects.

Marissa is very proud of the success of their program. "In 2013, eight of our devils were sent to Maria Island, a safe haven for them," she tells us, "and three were released on the Tasman Peninsula, behind a protective fence. They are all doing well."

Marissa also works in the field. Here she tracks a wild devil that has been collared using a portable antenna in northwest Tasmania.

What I learned:
It is possible to raise Tasmanian devils in captivity and release them successfully into the wild. There are a number of places in Australia that are breeding healthy devils for the insurance population. Another version of the devil facial tumor has shown up in the southeast of Tasmania; researchers think tumor diseases might be a normal occurrence in this species.

Learning to Get Along

One of the biggest challenges with captive populations of animals that might one day be returned to the wild is how best to manage them so that they develop their natural behaviors. In the wild, the mother devil leaves her young when they are about nine months old. The youngsters have grown up together, played together, and explored their environment together. Devils have very sensitive noses and can smell a carcass from at least 0.62 miles (1 kilometer) away, often joining other devils to feed. While they may compete sometimes for food, they will also cooperate in tearing a carcass apart. It's important that devils born in captivity are raised in ways that will make them comfortable around others of their kind.

To learn how best to rear captive devils, Marissa and her crew experimented with socializing the youngsters. They kept groups of three young devils together in enclosures for six weeks, then opened up the gates so that six individuals shared a pen. They found that the animals all accepted one another and were more active when six were together than when there were just three. The animals that had been socialized together in the groups of three would den together rather than with the animals they met later. They all got along, but they kept their earlier close relationships. This is now the standard way the young are socialized, with as little human contact as possible.

Like young devils at Healesville, these youngsters at Trowunna Wildlife Preserve grow up together, which helps them develop the social skills they will need as adults.

CHAPTER FOUR
Where Devils Live Wild

Our visit to Healesville Sanctuary allowed us to meet devils like Tierney and Sassafrass, devoted devil caretakers like Kathy Starr and Peter Comber, as well as dedicated researcher Marissa Parrott. We enjoyed the whole experience. But now I'm eager to head to Tasmania, where I will meet people involved in the Save the Tasmanian Devil Program and scientists doing research, and I will experience the wild Tasmanian environment myself.

I'm delighted that Jenny, John, and their grandson Felix are joining Greg and me on this adventure. We fly into the second largest city in Tasmania, Launceston, and are greeted in the airport lobby by an oversize devil statue, mouth open, pleading for contributions to the Save the Tasmanian Devil Appeal, the public fundraiser for the Save the Tasmanian Devil Program. I'm happy to feed it $20 Australian.

We start with a detour to Low Head, by the mouth of the Tamar River, where we watch tiny fairy penguins waddle their way out of the ocean, onto the rocks, and up to their nests for the night. Then we drive into Launceston proper, where Jenny and I visit Rebecca Cuthill, manager of the Save the Tasmanian Devil Appeal.

We enjoyed watching the fairy penguins, like this pair, waddle their way from the ocean to their nests in the dark.

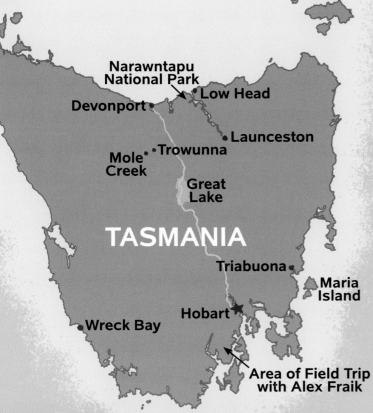

We flew into Launceston, then drove to Low Head for a couple of nights. After visiting Launceston, Narawntapu National Park and Trowunna, we stayed in Devonport before driving south across the middle of Tasmania to Hobart, where we stayed while visiting the area. I've also labeled Wreck Bay, where Carolyn Hogg and her group trapped and sampled devils in December of 2017.

This sign at the entrance to Narawntapu National Park warns visitors to slow down to 40 km (25 mph) and watch out for wildlife.

ENDANGERED

40

Progress and Problems

We walk into the lobby of Rebecca's office, where a beautiful poster of a devil hangs; it was created by a visiting artist from Japan. Rebecca explains the complications of the devil recovery effort. Many different organizations, including the Australian federal and Tasmanian state governments, zoo organizations, private wildlife parks, the University of Tasmania, and others, need to cooperate and coordinate their efforts to help the Tasmanian devil survive and recover.

"All the Tasmanian devils are managed by the Tasmanian government, which is very supportive," Rebecca says. "It's the government devil program at the end of the day that makes the decisions about what happens on the ground to the devils. That's David Pemberton's department."

I'm glad that I have an appointment to talk with him later this week.

She explains that a major focus of the devil program is the vaccine research. Hearing this, I smile, knowing that I'll also be spending time with Greg Woods at the Menzies Institute, learning more about the vaccine. Jenny has set me up well to learn about this complicated story.

Rebecca goes on, "We started releasing vaccinated devils in a couple of sites, including Narawntapu National Park, where the disease is present, in September of 2015. Devil numbers there were low, but it's perfect devil habitat, so we released twenty devils there with the trial vaccine. All those devils were given four shots and a booster shot as well. The few devils they have been able to recapture show no sign of the disease as of now, a year later."

Time will tell how effective the vaccine is. But meanwhile, Rebecca sums up with one vision of the future. "We might end up with an environment where the disease is present but there are vaccinated devils along with unvaccinated ones. Even at risk of disease, we need a wide genetic diversity present rather than having only a few devils out there."

Jenny and I say farewell and thank Rebecca for her time and all the useful information she's provided. Then we meet up with Greg, John, and Felix for lunch, and they tell us about the great museum they just visited.

Narawntapu National Park

Before leaving the United States, I thought Narawntapu National Park might be a great place to see Australian wildlife, and now I knew that devils had been released there. The five of us head out in our rental van in the afternoon. We've been dealing with rainy weather, and poorly labeled roads send us in the wrong direction, so I'm relieved and excited to see the sign for the park, along with a speed limit sign warning of the presence of devils here. I hoped the cold and gray weather might mean we'd see some wildlife. We park the van and follow a trail to a little bridge over a creek. Just across the bridge, a female Bennett's wallaby grazes. As we look closer, we see a baby, called a joey, peeking out from her pouch, looking at us. What a great sight! Up to this point, the only "wild" wildlife we'd seen was a gang of kangaroos on the river trail near Jenny's home. I have high hopes for more sightings here in Narawntapu, but no expectation of seeing devils, which are unlikely to show up until dark.

Once the wallaby grazes her way past the bridge, we feel okay crossing over. The trail seems to disappear into a wet meadow, where a number of female wallabies, each with a rounded pouch encasing a joey, graze. A few Tasmanian pademelons join in. These marsupials are darker and smaller than the Bennett's wallabies, and more skittish; they also have more rounded features and thinner tails.

We're delighted to see this mother wallaby and her joey so close to us.

These wallabies ignore us as we quietly walk past them.

You can see how pademelons differ from wallabies, with their thinner tails and darker color.

I keep in front of the group, wanting to experience an Australian forest, so different from what's familiar to me, on my own. The heavy rains of recent days have saturated the ground, and we pass by a landscape of twisted and skinny eucalyptus trees sprouting out of reflective swampy water—totally alien to my wild world experiences. Unfamiliar but lovely calls from hidden birds accentuate the feeling of other-ness as I hike. Expectant as I am at

every turn of seeing something new, the only wildlife that shows itself are more pademelons tucked into the underbrush and a lone kangaroo.

By the time we return to the car, darkness is quickly descending, and just past the park entrance are more road signs warning of devils. Evening

is a very dangerous time of day for these vulnerable creatures, as that's when they come out to socialize and feed on roadkill, often getting hit by cars themselves.

What I learned:
Many institutions in Australia have joined the effort to save and protect the Tasmanian devil. The wilds of Australia look very different from those of the United States and they are very beautiful.
I'm falling in love with this country.

The entrance to Trowunna Wildlife Preserve is hard to miss.

CHAPTER FIVE
Tasmanian Devils in Action

I'm thankful that the weather has improved as I'm eager to visit Trowunna Wildlife Preserve. Rebecca Cuthill called Androo Kelly, the preserve's director, "the devil whisperer," so I am looking forward to getting his perspective on the devils and their situation. Besides, Trowunna is home to more than sixty devils of all ages, living in enclosures with varied habitats for the animals to explore. Androo has worked with sixteen generations of devils since 1986, long before DFTD showed up, so he has long-term experience with these unique animals.

We drive to Trowunna through sheep-dotted farmlands drenched in bright green from the heavy but nourishing rainfall. A giant Tasmanian devil statue shows us where to turn. The location is like an oasis within the forest, with a sloping open meadow where kangaroos lazily lounge. My windbreaker holds back the mist and my waterproof shoes keep my feet dry as we walk across the wet, squishy ground.

Androo stands inside a fenced enclosure, demonstrating devil feeding behavior to a small group of people. He swings a kangaroo haunch in his right hand as three female devils that are no longer used for breeding trot out from their den. Each grabs one part of the haunch in her powerful jaws and a tug-of-war ensues, with all three devils chewing and pulling strenuously. Bit by bit, they tear off pieces of skin and meat as Androo explains their feeding habits. The devils, completely engrossed in their struggle, pay no attention to Androo or to us. A fourth devil hovers tentatively at the den entrance, seemingly fearful as she peers wistfully at the meat.

Androo explains that little was known about devil behavior twenty years ago, before the tumor disease appeared. Since then, we've learned a lot about the animals and the disease. He points out that the devil's behavior helps the disease spread when the animals bite one another while feeding or during mating encounters. I notice scars on the backs and rumps of these females as they grab and pull at the haunch. Finally, the seemingly timid devil sees her opportunity to join the fray. She gains control of the prized meat and runs off with it. Smart devil.

After the demo, we exchange introductions with Androo. He tells me that we're lucky. It had been raining there constantly for three days and just stopped two or three hours before we arrived. Androo takes me around, showing me the various devil enclosures and talking about his long association with these animals.

He describes his own relationship with the devils. "When I was a child in the 1950s, you hardly ever heard or even saw a Tasmanian devil," he explains. "I knew scary stories about them. The stories made you quite fearful. But I was always curious about the animal, and when I finally got to spend time with the devil, my views changed. To watch and study is the way to get to know something.

"I learned that the Tasmanian devil is actually a supersensitive, shy animal that would prefer to avoid confrontation. When they get together, they sound like they are trying to kill one another, but they are not. One finds the food by smell, then another finds it, and others join in. Their job is to clean up the sick, dead, dying animals to stop spreading disease."

Androo has had devils at Trowunna since before the disease appeared. He has shown others, such as Menna Jones, how best to keep them and how to breed them in captivity. Each pen is quite large, with a nice variety of surfaces, vegetation, cover, texture, etc., to help keep the animals from getting bored. These three breeding enclosures are grouped so that all of them can be viewed from a small, covered shack right next to them. As at Healesville Sanctuary, a male and a female are placed in adjacent pens and watched. If they seem to be interested in each other, they are put together and carefully observed. It's a tricky situation—if the female doesn't like the male, she will chase him away. If they get along, the male will dominate her, biting her back, dragging her around, and then keeping her sequestered in his den for days.

"The world to me is a laboratory," says Androo, who clearly has a special feeling for the devils and has studied them closely. He recognizes twenty-six different sounds they make, so he knows that vocal communication is important for the species. He says they don't really bite all that much while arguing over food; mostly they vocalize and open their mouths wide, displaying their gleaming white teeth, to intimidate one another. This pose—a menacing open mouth showing four sharp fangs—was, historically, the typical devil image displayed to the public. Androo says he was the first person to publish an image of a devil with its mouth closed!

He comments on their abundant long whiskers, pointing out that devils even have them on their necks. He thinks the whiskers may not just be organs of touch; they may sense vibrations of some sort. When devils sniff, they also bob their heads in quick little nods in a way I haven't seen in other animals. Perhaps they are using their whiskers as sensors when they do this.

These year-old devils are practicing opening their mouths wide in warning as they will do when they grow up.

You can see the long whiskers on the side of this devil's head.

A large, lushly vegetated enclosure is home to a number of devils young enough to get along together. From a distance, we see the animals lounging along the edge of a log. When they see us approach, they perk their ears and the group breaks up. A couple of them come closer to the fence to check us out.

After our tour, Androo refers us to his assistant, Drew, so we can get photos with a young devil. Drew brings out a beautiful black baby devil wrapped in a soft blue blanket and tells us how to hold it, warning that it might bite if it doesn't like how it's being handled. I get to hold it first and I'm careful to be gentle. Jenny and Felix both get a turn, but by then Drew is concerned that the little guy could be getting cold, so he takes it back to safety. We say our goodbyes and head off down the road, full of affection and gratitude both for the devils and for Androo and Drew and the respectful and nourishing care they take with these special creatures.

Devils have an excellent sense of smell.

What I learned:
The Tasmanian devil is actually not a frightening, aggressive animal, despite its big strong teeth and the scary sounds it makes. Androo is an expert on devils and sees them as intelligent, curious, and often social animals with acute senses.

CHAPTER SIX

Into the Heart of Devil Rescue

Time to head south. Instead of taking Route 1, the freeway that connects the north end of the island with Hobart, we take Highway A5, which climbs up into the wild and dramatic mountains called the Great Western Tiers, then winds down to follow the western shore of Great Lake, which lies almost at the center of the island.

We settle in at our hotel in Hobart, where so much of the Tasmanian devil research takes place at the University of Tasmania and at the Menzies Institute for Medical Research. David (nicknamed Doozie) Pemberton, director of the Save the Tasmanian Devil Program, also has his office nearby, and I'm eager to hear his thoughts.

Doozie doesn't just sit behind a desk. He also goes out in the field, as he's doing here, releasing a devil into the wild.

The wombat is a common animal in Australia.
We saw this mother and baby on Maria Island.

Learning the Long View

Doozie takes time from his very busy schedule to welcome me, Greg, and Jenny into his office to learn his perspective on the devil and the programs to save it.

He shows us some videos that demonstrate the adaptable nature of the Tasmanian devil. "They are so versatile," he remarks as the video shows a devil climbing a tree, chasing a possum. "They are like a bear, a little sun bear." Next, he pulls up a video of a devil struggling to cross a bridge. "They use their tail, they use their chin; that's how they get across the bridge. They are just determined." Another video shows a devil swimming, pausing to take a breath, and diving under a pipe in her way. "They can swim. She just took a breath and duck-dived under the pipe. We didn't realize they could do that."

The devil is able to climb trees.

This screenshot of a video shows a devil that's determined to cross a bridge.

Devils often crowd in together to feed. You can see the scars on these devils from earlier encounters.

Next Doozie sweeps his hand over a map of Tasmania, showing how many environments the devils can live in. "They don't go high in the forest. Anywhere else on the island you'll find devils."

The ideal habitat for devils is landscape that's broken up by fields, meadows, forests, and streams. "The magic is how far apart the areas of bush are. A devil will cross up to 300 meters [328 yards] of open space," he explains. "You have a forest and a creek. If there's bush along the creek, they'll follow it. But if the space is 500 meters [about a third of a mile] or more wide, they won't cross.

"Devils don't bite each other that often. They're actually quite docile. They're famous around the world because they scream and shout at each other, and that's all about *not* biting. The more they shout, the less chance they will bite because they're having an argument and they move on. They're kind of designed to have this ritualized encounter. Possibly once or twice a year a devil will bite another devil. That's not enough for the way the disease has spread through the population in just two years.

"When a devil loses the shouting match and turns around and runs, that's when it gets bitten. Maybe then the disease travels to the face."

I think about the devils we've seen at both Healesville and Trowunna. The adults often had obvious scars on their rear ends, but their faces had few marks of injury.

Doozie goes on with a couple of other ideas. "When they're feeding, they get up close, and it's possible the tumor cells rub off. There's all that close contact. And when a mother weans her young, she's nipping at them all the time. This could help explain why the disease gets across the population."

Doozie leaves me with much to think about—how much we've learned about this adaptable and intelligent species, and how our increased knowledge has shown us that the devil is a survivor by nature.

Journey to Part of the Solution

Marissa Parrott at Healesville Sanctuary had mentioned releasing devils on Maria Island, and David Pemberton also talked about the island's importance as a safe place with no dangerous vehicles or other threats to rewilded devils from the insurance populations. Captive-born animals are released on Maria Island and, if necessary, provided with food as they learn bit by bit how to survive on their own in the wild. Then their wild-born offspring are transplanted to the big island of Tasmania, to help with repopulation.

Maria Island was always high on my to-see list, and when Doozie explained its importance to the devil program, I was glad I'd scheduled a visit for the one empty day on our Hobart calendar. John and Felix have returned home, so Jenny joins me and Greg to drive to Triabunna, where we catch the 9:00 AM ferry to Maria Island. We won't have long—the return ferry departs at 3:30 PM, so we make the most of the time we have here by heading right out on the island's trails, soaking up this atmosphere of reprieve and renewal for the devils.

We pass by the old buildings now used by overnight campers. Hefty Cape Barren geese strut around, some in courting pairs. I have to remind myself that it's springtime here, not fall as it is at home!

The large Cape Barren goose is native to southern Australia.

Soon we enter a forest of towering eucalyptus, ferny tangles, and old paperbark tree giants. As we start seeing clearings in the forest, we encounter wombats. I enjoy watching

Paperbark giant

50

Ferny tangles

This den is probably being used by either a wombat or a Tasmanian devil.

This footprint on the muddy trail indicates that a devil passed by here not very long ago; below is the right front paw of a captive devil.

these rotund creatures with short legs as they graze their way across the landscape. I've learned that wombats are excellent den diggers, and devils often move into empty wombat dens. Where the forest becomes dense again, we keep a close eye out for signs of devils, even though we know we probably won't see the animals till evening. Jenny points out a particularly promising burrow under a log that almost certainly houses a wombat or a devil. I walk ahead of Greg and Jenny as we turn onto a trail that keeps to the forest rather than heading toward the cliffs. I spot a giant tree hollowed out at the base—it looks like a good place for a den. I leave the trail to check it out and pick my way up the

slope. It turns out to hold not a den but rather a nest of an ambitious species of ant that makes big mounds. I join Greg and Jenny farther along the trail, and they show me a nice surprise. On the section of the trail I missed, they've found a very clear footprint that might be from a devil. Later on, we show a photo of it to Menna Jones, and she says yes, it's the right front footprint of an adult devil, and it's quite fresh. A devil must have passed this way the previous night.

I can see why the devils do well on this island. Most of it is wild forest and meadows traversed by hiking paths, and the only motorized vehicle is a forest service truck that, when used, crawls slowly along the rough old

road. Without cars, the main danger for the devils, and with abundant food like wombats available, the devils' success here is understandable.

The eucalyptus forest is a perfect habitat for devils.

We eat our sandwiches at a picnic table tucked into a protected spot under the trees. The wind gets cold and brings showery bits of rain, but we are content in our peaceful spot— the quiet only interrupted by the croaking of frogs and the whisper of the wind in the trees. As we resume our journey and go back to the visitors' center, however, the rain gets more and more insistent as the wind picks up. By the time we get there we have to shed our wet outer layers. A video called *Aussie Animal Island* is showing in the visitors' center. It chronicles the introduction of devils to the island and follows a woman who raised three baby devils whose mother had been killed on the road. Researchers released two of these youngsters, when they were fully grown, onto Maria Island, which did not have a devil population before the Save the Tasmanian Devil Program releases and so did not have DFTD. They trapped one of them again months later. She had not only sur-

People who just arrived at the dock are getting ready to move onto Maria Island. Soon we get on the boat for our turbulent trip back to mainland Tasmania.

vived but had bred and had four swollen teats, meaning four babies waited in her den. Later, they brought the woman who had raised the orphaned devils to the island so she could see how her baby had grown up and was contributing to the devil population.

As the boat arrives with afternoon visitors who will all be spending the night, a giant squall hits, with piercing spikes of rain flying horizontally with the wind, making the trek to the boat extremely unpleasant. I feel for the arriving folks who are struggling to load their gear onto carts and probably wondering what crazy idea led them to decide to camp out on this island.

The boat ride back feels like a fine Disneyland creation, which is how I view it so I can pretend it's pleasant. It really is kind of fun, though, since the bow-slamming rock and roll of the boat fortunately isn't the kind that leads to nausea.

What I learned:
As Androo said, the devils don't actually bite one another over food access as much as researchers had once thought. The tumor cells might rub off the face of an infected devil onto another individual while they are feeding. Devils are highly intelligent, learn easily from experience, and might be able to survive in the wild even as the disease persists. They can adapt to a variety of environments.

A Tasmanian devil named Sparrow breathes in oxygen from the anesthesia cone after having his blood sampled.

CHAPTER SEVEN
Developing a Vaccine

The Save the Tasmanian Devil Program has high hopes for the development of a vaccine against DFTD. If the research succeeds, it could provide information and techniques useful in fighting human cancers as well. As we've learned, DFTD can ravage its victims because their immune cells don't recognize the cancer cells as "other," so these cells just keep dividing and dividing until they kill the host. And in the meantime, chances are that the victim has passed DFTD cells on to other devils, perpetuating the cycle and devastating the devil population.

I've looked forward to visiting with cancer researcher Greg Woods to see how he's doing with his important work. After meeting him in his office, we travel to the town of Richmond, where some experimental devils are kept on a farm. Their pens are smaller than those at Trowunna, but they vary in architecture to provide the animals with some variety in their surroundings.

Adam and Sparrow each live in a small pen that has varied structure to provide some variety in the environment.

Awakening the Immune System

Scientists like Anne-Maree and Jenny were amazed when they realized that the reason DFTD was so easily passed on was because healthy devils' immune systems didn't recognize the tumor cells as something "other," like an infection, something to be fought and killed in order to maintain the animal's health. Their immune systems just ignored the tumors, which could then keep growing and growing and being passed on to other unfortunate devils. When a person gets a transplant of a new body organ, such as a kidney, from another person, doctors give the person drugs that suppress, or weaken, their immune system so it won't reject the new kidney. If the patient who receives the kidney doesn't take the antirejection drugs, his or her body will recognize that the kidney has not always been there and will destroy it. But the devils' immune systems don't respond to the tumor cells even though they came from another devil's body. What's going on here?

It's taken lots of cooperation among scientists at the Menzies Institute and other laboratories in Australia, England, and Denmark to find the surprising answer. The way the immune system recognizes foreign cells is by sensing the presence of major histocompatibility complex (MHC) molecules on the surface of the cells. These molecules tell the immune system whether the cell is healthy, diseased, or foreign. The DFTD cells don't have these molecules on their surface, so the immune system can't detect them. It's as if they were wearing invisibility cloaks. However, the tumor cells do have the genes that code for the MHC molecules, it's just that the genes are turned off. Scientists have found a way to turn the genes back on, giving the researchers a chance to find a way to trigger an immune response in the devils' blood.

Using tumor cells that have the MHC genes turned back on, the team has been able to produce a sort of vaccine that stimulates a devil's immune system to create antibodies to fight the foreign cells. It doesn't work like a true vaccine, but it does get the devil's blood cells to produce antibodies. It's now being tested by releasing immunized devils into the wild.

We arrive just as it's time to take blood samples from devils Adam and Sparrow. The scientists are testing compounds called adjuvants that were added to immunizations (shots) to help "wake up" the devils' immune systems. These devils were given the experimental immunization some weeks ago in the hope that the combination will stimulate their immune systems to make antibodies on their own. Then, two weeks ago, Adam and Sparrow were given an injection of the antigen the scientists want their immune systems to react to. The scientists will check the blood that's being drawn today to see if these devils' systems have produced antibodies in response to the antigen.

Veterinarians Ruth Pye and Alexandre Kreiss will draw the blood samples. They trap the first devil, Adam, and transfer him to a table in a burlap bag. They locate his head within the bag, then place an anesthesia cone over his muzzle through the bag. They attach a monitor to Adam's ear to keep track of his heart rate. Once Adam is unconscious, Alexandre takes a blood sample. Alexandre checks Adam's gums to make sure they are nice and pink, indicating that the blood is flowing well. He shows us Adam's strong, impressive teeth—devils' canine teeth continue to grow throughout the animals' lives because they often break when they feed on bones. After the exam and blood draw, Alexandre gives Adam oxygen by way of the cone and massages him to help him wake up. Once Adam is awake, Alexandre and Ruth return him to his pen, watch to make sure he's okay, then move on to repeat the procedure with Sparrow. When the work is finished, the family that runs the farm gives us a taste of good fresh cider, then we head back to Hobart.

After luring Adam into a trap, Alex and Ruth transfer him to a burlap bag.

1. Ruth and Alex give Adam the anesthetic through the material of the burlap sack.

2. Alex uses a needle and syringe to take the blood sample.

3. He checks Adam's gums to make sure they are bright pink, which shows the blood is flowing nicely.

4. You can see the monitor in Adam's ear that makes sure his heart is beating properly as he gets oxygen from the cone.

5. Alex massages Adam to help him recover from the blood drawing procedure.

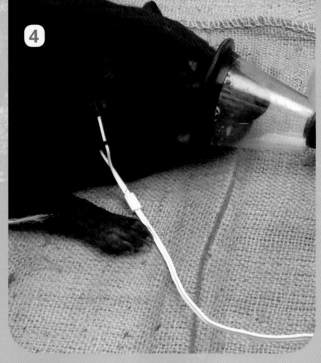

4

After lunch in town with Greg Woods and some students, I go with him to visit the lab. In order to participate in any lab activity, the rules require that you wear a lab coat, so I put one on. The concern is that you could spill something dangerous on your clothing in the lab, like a disease culture, and it could end up leaving the lab with you. Greg shows me the warm incubators where cultures of different kinds of devil cells are grown. He explains how important it is to maintain the correct temperature and humidity inside.

5

Here I am in a borrowed lab coat, all ready to see what goes on in the lab.

What I learned:
I learn later that both the immunization mixture given to Adam and the one tested on Sparrow stimulated their immune systems to make antibodies against an antigen after just one dose. While we watched, Adam and Sparrow were given second immunizations just like their first ones. Later, when their blood was sampled again, both animals had even more antibodies to the antigen in their blood. Now the scientists know that combining an antigen such as dead DFTD cells with these adjuvants can stimulate a strong immune response.

The incubators keep the cell cultures at the proper temperature to grow.

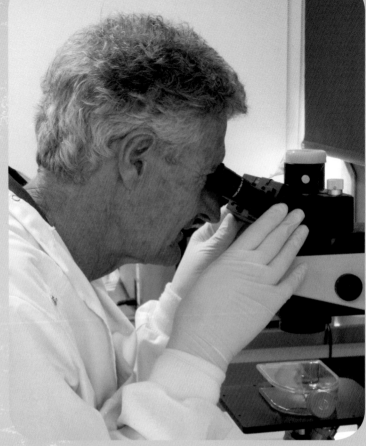

Greg puts a slide with some cells from one of the cultures under the microscope, then adjusts the focus for me.

He removes one of the cultures and quickly closes the incubator door. Then he puts the culture under the microscope and gets the cells in focus. "Here, take a look and let me know what you see," Greg says.

I sit down and adjust the focus a bit for my eyes. It feels good to be looking into a microscope in a lab once again—it's been a long time since I've done that!

"What do these cells look like?" Greg asks.

"They look pretty evenly spaced and connected to one another," I reply.

"Good," he responds. "These are normal connective tissue cells. Now I'll show you three other cultures."

The cells in the second culture don't look as connected but they still have an orderly appearance; these are normal Schwann cells. Next he shows me a third culture with more chaotic cells that don't seem to be connected; these cells come from the first type of devil facial tumor that was discovered, which originated in Schwann cells. Last, Greg shows me a chaotic culture of cells that do look connected; it consists of cells from the second kind of tumor, which began in a different type of tissue.

"I see why you were confused at first by the cells in the last culture when you saw them," I comment. "They definitely look different."

"Yes, that's when we suspected there was yet another kind of facial tumor out there," Greg answered.

Greg talks about his hopes of developing an effective vaccine that can help protect insurance-population devils from the disease when they are introduced back into the wild. There is only one way to find out if this treatment will work, and that is to use the vaccine on some animals and release them into places where they will be exposed to DFTD. "We realize we could be putting these animals at risk of getting sick if the vaccine doesn't work, but this is really our only way to find out whether it's effective or not," Greg says.

What I learned:
Scientists are working to develop an effective vaccine against DFTD. They hope to end up with a vaccine that will be effective after just one dose, but it isn't easy. Their research also has potential applications for fighting cancer in humans.

These slides are made from tissues of devils prepared for viewing with the microscope. After being preserved and sliced thinly, the tissues are treated with special stains that color tumor cells dark red.

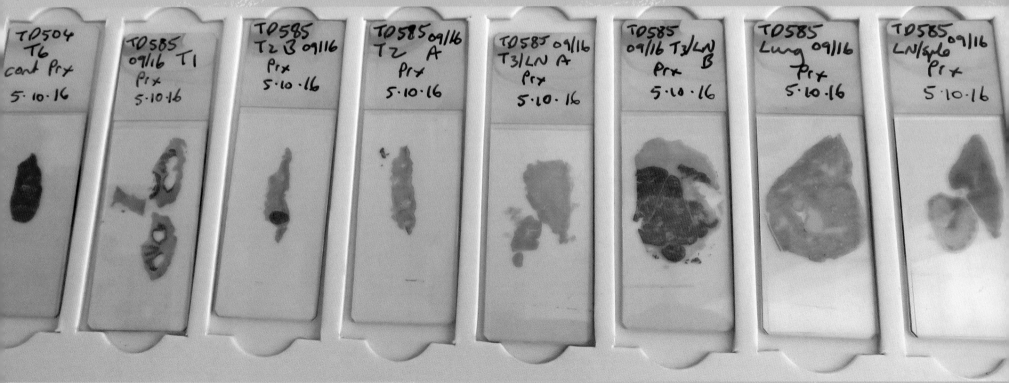

CHAPTER EIGHT

Adventure in the Wild

Near the end of our Tasmanian stay, I go into the field with Alex Fraik, a graduate student at Washington State University, and her volunteer assistant, Emily Burton. They are trapping devils on plots of private property in the hilly country south of Hobart to get data and samples. It's quite wild land except for near the houses. We ride in a big, bouncy university truck loaded with equipment. Its almost-bald tires have a hard time getting traction going up some of the hills on the narrow and unpaved roads, but Alex has lots of experience dealing with this challenge.

The sun shines down through the cool, clear spring air. Everything is damp from the recent rain, and breezes and birdsong make it very inviting. Alex is studying the genetics of both tumor diseases. Her specialty within genetics is called genomics, which uses modern technology to analyze genetic information to learn how genes function and interact with an animal's environment.

Alex sets her traps in the area where the second type of facial tumor was discovered. She needs to collect samples from healthy individuals and from those with one or the other of the diseases for her research. "I want to trap devils with cancer to learn more about it and help them," Alex says, "but I am sad because, when I do trap them, it just upsets me to see an animal in pain." No one likes to see animals suffering from such a cruel disease, but Alex needs the material for her work.

Rural Tasmania is a mixture of farms and forests, the kind of habitat favorable to Tasmanian devils.

This trap set by Alex has been tripped—now it's time to see if there's a Tasmanian devil inside.

What I learned:

The traps Alex has set are white plastic PVC tubes about 1 foot (30 centimeters) in diameter and 3 feet (91 centimeters) long. The traps were invented by Nick Mooney to make captured devils feel more secure, stop them from breaking teeth, which happens when they try to escape from steel mesh traps, and allow efficient cleaning after devil captures, which is very helpful for disease control. One end is blocked and the other has a hinged door that is triggered when the devil enters the tube to take a bait inside. The ends have holes and the sides have narrow slits so the devils get plenty of air.

After checking a few traps near the road that haven't been tripped, we drive down a narrow, muddy road and park near a cabin. Emily hikes through the forest and across a grassy field to check a trap at the forest's edge. The trap is closed, so she waves us over to join her. Alex checks the trap, standing it up, sliding the top back, and peering in to see what's inside. "It's not a devil, it's an eastern quoll," she says. "They also feed on carrion, so sometimes we end up catching them."

Alex puts a burlap bag over the trap and tips it over so the quoll slides into the bag. She takes some measurements for a colleague who is studying quolls, then she releases the animal, which runs away as fast as it can.

This time, a quoll took the bait, not a devil.

To reset the trap, Alex takes a piece of meat, ties it to a string, and lowers it inside the trap so it goes all the way to the bottom. Then she positions the trap deep into the underbrush, slides the door open, and sets the trigger so it will close if the bait is pulled.

Catching a Devil

We have better luck with the next trap. Alex checks it and finds a devil inside, so Emily gets busy setting up to record the identity of the animal and measurements and observations about it. Meanwhile, Alex uses a portable scanner to check the devil in the trap for a microchip. "No chip," she says. "We haven't caught this one before."

If there's no chip, part of the following procedure is to inject one, name the animal, and add it to their records. Just as with the quoll, Alex tips the trap and lets the devil slide gently into the bag so she can take measurements.

Unlike the captive devils that are used to people and active in the daytime, captured wild devils are usually very quiet. They don't struggle either; this one stays passive while Alex reaches in to check its gender. "It's a female," she says, and feels inside the pouch for young. "No babies here, but the teats are enlarged, so she's got babies waiting in a nearby den," Alex explains to me.

Alex lowers the bait into the trap, which is then set down and set.

Every time a trap is tripped, Alex's assistant has to set up for the examination of the devil and note-taking.

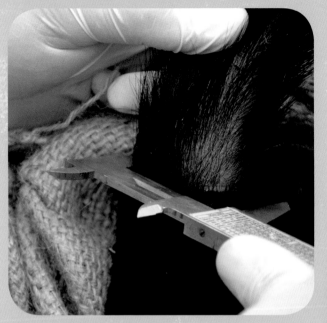

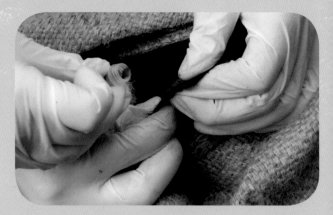

She also pricks a small vessel on one ear to get a blood sample.

The captured devil remains in the sack for the entire examination. When it's all over, Alex moves to the side of the work area, opens the sack, and the devil hightails it back to freedom.

Alex measures the devil's tail.

As she works, Alex calls out measurements and observations and Emily jots them down. Emily is one of several volunteers, but she and Alex work together so well it seems like they've been at it forever. While examining the devil, Alex pays special attention to her face to see if there are any signs of DFTD.

Once all the data is gathered, Alex carefully releases the devil.

Following the Trapline

Most of the remaining two dozen or so traps are empty. Some are close to the road so we can just stop briefly, check to see if the bait is still intact, and make sure the trap is still firing correctly. The second trapped devil is a male who is so quiet, at first Alex thinks he may be sound asleep. She pokes her head in the trap and says, "Oh, it's just Dean. He's always quiet when I get to the trap—that's his style! He's my favorite."

The third is a female with young in her pouch. "We can't risk disturbing her anymore," says Alex, "so I'll let her go." The young are quite big. Alex leaves the mother in the open sack on the ground and we walk away.

We stop at a country home that a married couple enjoys sharing with a devil family. Devils made a den under their house several years ago, and the couple has loved their devil neighbors ever since. The wife plays a video taken one night when the devils below were making all sorts of ghostly sounds. I don't see how these people can live with the noise, but they are delighted. They provided the devils with a piece of plastic pipe to use as an entrance to the den instead of squeezing under the edge of the house as they had before. In return, these folks have been able to watch baby devils romp and play in their yard; no wonder they are happy to share!

Our journey began at 7:00 AM and now it's late afternoon; time to head back to Hobart. Alex drops me off at my hotel, then she heads back to the lab to refrigerate the samples, centrifuge the blood, and record the data collected that day into the computer. Tomorrow she will be up early in the morning to check the traps once again—that's what it means to be a field research scientist.

A young devil runs for the tube leading to the den under the house.

What I learned:
Gathering data on wild devils takes time and effort.
The wild devils are very quiet and passive when handled.

This devil is part of a planned release into the wild.

CHAPTER NINE

Looking to the Future

Leaving Tasmania isn't easy—I met so many interesting and helpful people and learned so much fascinating information about the Tasmanian devil that I want to stay longer, but it's time to go.

I fly to Sydney for one last visit with devil scientists Dr. Katherine Belov, professor of comparative genomics, and Dr. Carolyn Hogg, research manager for the Australasian Wildlife Genomics Group at the University of Sydney. Both are involved in the Save the Tasmanian Devil Program (STDP). They emphasize some important points about what has been learned over time about making the devil recovery program a success. For example, the managers of the program always keep in mind the importance of maintaining what little genetic diversity the species has by carefully choosing which animals to breed.

Rewilding the Devils

Carolyn has also been a part of the team determining how best to get healthy devils back into the wild. The point of the program is not just to keep the species alive, but to help them recover their lives in the wild. As the largest remaining native marsupial carnivore, the devil plays important roles in the Tasmanian ecosystem.

We now know that devils raised and kept in large enclosures away from people do better when they are released into the wild than devils kept in smaller spaces with more exposure to human activity. Maria Island provides a great open environment for helping the species make the transition from captive to wild. As Carolyn points out, "There are no dogs, no disease, no cars on Maria Island, and there's plenty of food. Only one devil out of the first twenty-eight released there died, and he got crushed in a wombat burrow. All the others figured out how to survive in the wild. And all but one of the females went on to breed."

Devils from the insurance-population locations are often released on Maria Island, where they breed. Their young grow up wild and learn how to take care of themselves, then are transported and released to the species' main habitat on the island of Tasmania.

The recovery team knows the pedigrees of the animals and can choose which ones to release in any particular area on Tasmania to help maintain genetic diversity. Many released animals are equipped with GPS collars with reflective tape, so their movements can be tracked,

These devil footprints are from Maria Island.

providing important information about the success of the program. The reflective tape also makes them more visible to drivers in the dark.

Some devils are given what's called a "soft release." They are set free inside a fenced portion of their new home area so they can get used to it. They are also fed while they get familiarized with what wild foods are

Some devils are given GPS collars when they are released.

Scientist Dr. Judy Clarke releases a devil into a large fenced area, where it will begin to become acquainted with its new environment.

available. Other individuals undergo a "hard release." The transport tubes are opened, and the devils head out to explore their new homes.

Devil Updates

In July 2017, the Wild Devil Recovery Project (WDR), which is part of the STDP, reported on the progress of reintroductions. Up until then, 125 devils had been released into four different locations around Tasmania. The devils are in the greatest danger of being hit by cars in the first few weeks after release, so researchers now feed them away from roads to prevent them from being struck and help them adapt to their new homes. Signs also warn drivers to be careful and watch for devils. These measures are paying off. None of the thirty-three devils released in May 2017 in northeastern Tasmania were killed by cars.

In July 2017, three devils that had received the vaccine and been released in one recovery area were found to have small DFTD tumors. However, these same animals were trapped again in September and were doing well. The two males had put on weight, a good sign, and the female had young stashed in her den.

More recently, in February 2018, samples from the nineteen devils released in Narawntapu National Park and the thirty-three released at Stony Head, all of which had received immunizations, show that 95 percent of them had DFTD-specific antibodies in their blood. Now we know that devils *can* produce such antibodies. The scientists hope these antibodies will be able to keep the animals safe from DFTD.

Reconnecting with Alex and Menna

In September 2017, I travel to Pullman, Washington, to visit the lab of Dr. Andrew Storfer, where Alex Fraik is a graduate student. The lab's large group of students explores the genetics and genomics of the Tasmanian devil from a variety of angles. These scientists have as their resource a huge database of the genomes and other statistics about devils from years before DFTD appeared, thanks to Menna's many years of fieldwork.

Using this data, the young researchers can ask a variety of questions about changes in the genes of the devils to see what factors might influence their ability to survive the disease.

In early October, I'm delighted to host Menna, her husband, and their sons for lunch at our home in Montana while Menna is in the United States on a Fulbright Fellowship.

She tells me the latest news about the devil programs. Menna's field research is showing that even in the area where the disease began, some devils still survive. Is this because some of them have developed ways of fighting off the disease? Or have devils from other areas moved in?

One very promising finding is that a few diseased devils appear to have recovered, indicating the possibility of evolving disease resistance. I also learn from both Alex and Menna that the second tumor type hasn't been spreading very fast, probably because the devil population in the area where it started is scattered.

The Evolving Devil

In collaboration with Menna Jones's University of Tasmania team, scientists at Washington State University in Pullman, Washington, including Alex Fraik, and at the University of Idaho in nearby Moscow, Idaho, are working to pin down how the Tasmanian devil is adapting and evolving to the challenge of the fatal DFTD by studying the devil's genome. Evolution takes place in response to challenges and opportunities presented by environments. One term for this is "natural selection."

Ultimately, traits such as resistance to a disease only get passed on when an organism survives long enough to reproduce and therefore give to the next generation those particular adaptive genes that help its survival. And as Menna Jones says, "You can't have a stronger selection pressure than death, and nearly all devils die of DFTD within six months of developing tumors." When an animal dies before it has offspring, it can't pass its genes

on. When an animal reproduces before it dies, its genes are passed on and can help the next generation to survive. The frequency of those genes occurring in the population will increase as the generations continue.

One way the devil may be evolving to help it survive as a species is for the females to breed when they're young, before DFTD can kill them. Menna and her team have found that devils in areas with DFTD are indeed breeding and giving birth at a younger age than they did before the disease arrived.

Another way to see how the species could be changing is to track the genomes of trapped individuals over time. That's an approach being used by scientists like Alex, who gather tissue samples and compare the genomes of devils as they encounter DFTD. This requires long hours of intensive fieldwork and lab work, but it can contribute important information to our understanding of how animal species might manage to survive such serious challenges. The Washington

Alex in the middle of extracting RNA from samples in the lab.

State scientists continue to study devil genomes and have found some interesting results. For example, they've looked at 16,000 areas of the devils' genome and learned that, in females, up to 70 percent of the genetic variations they find appear to have some link to survival. Findings like this could be used to help select which devils to use in breeding programs.

Meanwhile, the Menzies Institute scientists found tumor-fighting antibodies in the blood of six wild devils that had developed DFTD, and the devils' tumors got smaller. This is exciting because it looks like some wild devils can develop the ability to fight off the disease.

Since then, trapping surveys of devils in certain areas are confirming that the species appears to be finding ways to survive this epidemic. Trapping in September 2018 found a number of healthy old devils in areas with DFTD, including one that previously had visible tumors but then showed no signs of the disease. The summary of findings from that survey concludes "Overall information gathered from our annual monitoring program has found that devils are persisting in the landscape and are coexisting with DFTD. It is now apparent that DFTD is part of the devils' ecology."

Menna Jones and Dorothy Patent in Dorothy's Montana front yard.

Learning about devil behavior in the wild is challenging, since the animals are active almost exclusively at night. While in Tasmania, I met briefly with Rodrigo Hamede, who ran a field study on devils and DFTD for ten years. He described how some devils have been trapped and given special collars that record interactions among individuals. By analyzing such data, scientists can learn more about the lives of these secretive animals in the wild.

Exploring for Devils

Much of Tasmania has been thoroughly settled, with cities, towns, and farmland. So far, DFTD hasn't reached the wilder, less populated northwestern part of the island. The mountainous southwest quarter of the island is even wilder, with several national parks penetrated by only a few hiking trails and one road. Until recently, we didn't know if devils lived there. But thanks to researcher Liz Murchison, who hiked the area, collected devil scat, and sent it to

Carolyn Hogg at the University of Sydney, we found out that the region is in fact inhabited by devils.

To learn more, scientists from the STDP, the University of Sydney (USYD), and Toledo Zoo (including STDP team leader from Toledo Dr. Samantha Fox), and Carolyn spent eight days exploring the southwest wilderness on a successful quest to find and trap devils. Here's what Carolyn wrote in an email after they returned:

The trip to SW Tasmania was amazing. The coast is very wild and remote. There were two trapping teams of five people who went to Wreck Bay and Nye Bay on the SW coast. We were helicoptered in with all our equipment and spent 8 days camping in the field. I was on the Nye Bay team where we hiked over 100 km in soft sand for the week, carrying the large PVC pipe traps on our backs. We managed to create a trapline which was 10 km long from north to south. We trapped 14 devils between the two teams

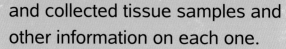

and collected tissue samples and other information on each one.

The exciting news was that we did not find any signs of disease, and we found older animals up to five years old as well as breeding females. So we are now able to say that there are two known disease-free populations in Tasmania, in the far NW in Woolnorth and in the SW.

Beyond Tasmania

As the recovery program and the research associated with it continue, we are learning information that might be helpful far beyond Tasmania. For example, working with devils got Kathy Belov curious about how the young in the pouch remain healthy, despite the environment they could be exposed to as their mothers dig burrows in the dirt and feed on carrion.

The pouch where they grow does open to the back (away from these environmental hazards), but still, their environment could introduce dangerous bacteria or viruses into the pouch. Now Kathy's lab has found that the devil mother's milk and the lining of the pouch contain molecules that are antibiotic and possibly even anti-cancer agents.

The research at the Menzies Institute on how to wake up the immune system to the presence of DFTD cells and fight them could be promising in the treatment of cancer in humans as well.

For me, traveling to Australia had been a dream wish. Being able not only to spend time with my friend Jenny, meet her family, and see some of the sights, but also to visit with so many devoted scientists working hard in the lab and the field to learn about

the Tasmanian devil has been a great gift. I left the United States fearing that this iconic animal could be wiped out in the wild within my lifetime, but I returned home with confidence that this will not happen.

Between the teams of researchers, volunteers, field scientists, and all the others involved in saving the devil, as well as the devil's own toughness and ability to evolve and survive adversity, I'm confident that Australia's largest marsupial carnivore, head of nature's cleanup crew, will survive and even thrive in the wilds of Australia's largest island. I think back about the big devil statue at the Launceston Airport, asking travelers to feed it money to help save the species through the Save the Tasmanian Devil Appeal. I gave it just $20 Australian, and when Rebecca Cuthill told me that the Appeal has distributed more than $3 million Australian over the last six years, I know that Australian citizens as well as visitors to this beautiful country care about the future of this special and unique animal.

It's looking like the Tasmanian devil may
be moving toward a sunnier future.

ACKNOWLEDGMENTS

I couldn't have experienced this great adventure without the generous gifts of time and attention from the many people named in this book who have been devoted to learning about and caring for these fascinating animals. Thanks also to Bruce Lyons, who helped with my queries about the immunization program after Greg Woods retired. Despite their busy lives, they shared their time and knowledge with me so I could share this story with my readers. Thank you all!

GLOSSARY

Adjuvant: A substance that helps activate the immune system as part of an immunization.

Antibody: A protein in the blood made by the immune system that attacks an antigen.

Antigen: A substance that stimulates the blood to produce an antibody against it.

Carrion: The decaying flesh of dead animals.

Chromosomes: Structures carrying the DNA which makes up genes. They occur in pairs in the nucleus of the cells of most plants and animals. One of each pair comes from the father and the mother.

DNA: The chemical that makes up genes. It is a long molecule, whose sequence of four components makes up the genetic code that determines the function of the genes.

Ecologist: A scientist who studies the interactions of living things with one another and with the environment where they live.

Geneticist: A scientist who studies genetics.

Genetics: The study of how traits are passed on from one generation to another.

Genome: The collection of all the genes of any particular species.

Genomics: A special area of study within genetics that analyzes all of an organism's DNA and looks for changes in structure, function, and evolution of genetic information over time as the environment varies.

Immunization: Providing a vaccine or similar substance to stimulate the immune system to fight disease.

Major histocompatibility complex (MHC): Molecules that normally appear on the cell surface and are recognized as "other," stimulating the immune system to make antibodies.

TO LEARN MORE

Books

Owen, David, and David Pemberton, *Tasmanian Devil: A Unique and Threatened Animal.* Sydney, Australia: Allen & Unwin, 2012.

Internet Resources

Save the Tasmanian Devil Program homepage: www.tassiedevil.com.au/tasdevil.nsf

Save the Tasmanian Devil Program on Facebook: www.facebook.com/SavetheTasmanianDevilProgram

Short video showing capture and release of devils: www.youtube.com/watch?v=mQ74R7oMCGE

Brief video that summarizes the devil's situation as of 2015: www.youtube.com/watch?v=zXx-g31J22c

SOURCES

Chapter 1

Deakin, Janine E., H. S. Bender, A. M. Pearse, J. A. Graves, et al. "Genomic Restructuring in the Tasmanian Devil Facial Tumour: Chromosome Painting and Gene Mapping Provide Clues to Evolution of a Transmissible Tumour" *PLOS Genetics* 8, no. 2 (Feb. 2012): 1–16.

Deakin, Janine, video conference and recorded interview with the author, Sept. 23, 2016.

Graves, Jenny, unpublished memoir and personal conversations with the author, 2015–17.

Jones, Menna, recorded, in-person interview with the author, Oct. 6, 2016.

Owen, David, and David Pemberton, *Tasmanian Devil: A Unique and Threatened Animal.* Sydney, Australia: Allen & Unwin, 2012.

Chapter 2

Cronin, Leonard, *Cronin's Key Guide to Australian Mammals.* Sydney, Australia: Allen & Unwin, 2008.

Owen, David, and David Pemberton, *Tasmanian Devil: A Unique and Threatened Animal.* Sydney, Australia: Allen & Unwin, 2012.

Chapter 3

Author's tour of Healesville Sanctuary facility with Kathy Starr.

Comber, Peter and Marissa Parrott, recorded, in-person interviews with the author at Healesville Sanctuary, Sept. 21, 2016.

Epstein, Brendan, M. Jones, R. Hamede, et al. "Rapid evolutionary response to a transmissible cancer in Tasmanian Devils," *Nature Communications* (Aug. 30, 2016).

Chapter 4

Cuthill, Rebecca, recorded, in-person interview with the author in Launceston, Sept. 28, 2016.

Chapter 5

Kelly, Androo, recorded, in-person interview with the author at Trowunna Wildlife Preserve, Oct. 1, 2016.

Chapter 6

Pemberton, David, recorded, in-person interview with the author in Hobart, Oct. 4, 2016.

Chapter 7

Lyons, Bruce, email exchanges with the author, Jan. 2018.

Patchett, Amanda L., C. Tovar, L. M. Corcoran, A. B. Lyons, and G. M. Woods. "The toll-like receptor ligands Hiltonol® (polyICLC) and imiquimod effectively activate antigen-specific immune responses in Tasmanian devils (*Sarcophilus harrisii*)." *Developmental and Experimental Immunology*, 76 (Nov. 2017.): 352–60.

Pye, Ruth, R. Hamede, H. V. Siddle, A. Caldwell, et al. "Demonstration of immune responses against devil facial tumour disease in wild Tasmanian devils," *Biology Letters*, Oct. 12, 2016, dx.doi.org/10.1098/rsbl.2016.0553.

Tovar, Cesar C., R. J. Pye, A. Kreiss, G. M. Woods, et al. "Regression of devil facial tumour disease following immunotherapy in immunised Tasmanian devils," *Scientific Reports (Nature)*, March 9, 2017.

Woods, Greg, recorded, in-person interview with the author in Hobart, Oct. 7, 2016.

Chapter 8

Fraik, Alex, in-person and email discussions with the author.

Chapter 9

Author's visit to laboratory of Andrew Storfer and his students at Washington State University, Sept. 6, 2017.

Belov, Kathy and Carolyn Hogg, recorded, in-person interviews with the author in Sydney, Oct. 10, 2016.

Epstein, et al., 2016

Fraik, Alex, Menna Jones, Bruce Lyons, and Rebecca Cuthill emails with author.

Pye, Ruth, A. Patchett, E. A. Silva, M. J. Marten, et al. "Immunization strategies producing a humoral IgG immune response against devil facial tumor disease in the majority of Tasmanian devils destined for wild release," *Frontiers in Immunology*, 9, Article 259, Feb. 2018, www.researchgate.net/publication/323264067.

Updates from Save the Tasmanian Devil Program at www.tassiedevil.com.au/tasdevil.nsf.

Scientific Publications

Deakin, et al., 2012.

Epstein, et al., 2016.

Lazenby, Billie T., M. W. Tobler, W. E. Brown, C. E. Hawkins, et al. "Density trends and demographic signals uncover the long-term impact of transmissible cancer in Tasmanian devils," *Journal of Applied Ecology* (Feb. 5, 2018). doi.org/10.1111/1365-2664.13088.

Patchett, et al., 2017.

Pye, et al., 2016.

Tovar, et al., 2017.

The Save the Tasmanian Devil Program Appeal provides a way for people to donate to the program.

Photo Credits

Index

SCIENTISTS IN THE FIELD

Where Science Meets Adventure

Check out these titles to meet more scientists
who are out in the field—and contributing every
day to our knowledge of the world around us:

Looking for even more adventure? Craving updates on the work of your favorite scientists, as well as in-depth
video footage, audio, photography, and more? Then visit the Scientists in the Field website!

sciencemeetsadventure.com